Feng Shui for Success

Achieving Your Goals and Fulfilling Your Dreams

By

Skylar MeiWu

Table of Content

Introduction to Feng Shui 2

The Basics of Feng Shui for Success 9

Feng Shui Tips for Your Office or Workplace 15

Feng Shui Tips for Your Home 23

Feng Shui Tips for Your Finances 30

Feng Shui Tips for Your Career 42

Feng Shui Tips for Your Personal Growth 53

Feng Shui Tips for Success in Relationships 63

Feng Shui Tips for Mental and Emotional Well-being 73

Putting it All Together 82

Conclusion and Action Steps 91

Introduction to Feng Shui

Feng Shui, an ancient Chinese philosophy rooted in the harmonious interplay of natural forces, has garnered significant attention in recent times. It postulates that the arrangement and orientation of elements in one's surroundings can profoundly impact the flow of life energy or "Qi," thereby influencing overall well-being, prosperity, and success. In this context, a Feng Shui book focused on the theme of success has emerged as a highly sought-after resource, entwining practical wisdom with transcendent principles.

Delving into the success-oriented Feng Shui tome, one uncovers a treasure trove of insights that elucidate the intricate relationship between the spatial organization and personal achievement. The book elucidates how deft manipulation of the environment, following the tenets of this time-honored doctrine, can engender a positive energy that nurtures success in various spheres of life.

The book's compelling narrative is augmented by the author's adroit employment of less conventional linguistic expressions, making it a truly engaging read. This literary finesse, coupled with the practical applicability of the book's contents, resonates deeply with readers who seek to unravel the secrets of attaining triumph through ancient wisdom.

Furthermore, the book explores the subtle complexities of Feng Shui by examining the interplay of the five elements - wood, fire, earth, metal, and water - and the Bagua, an octagonal diagram embodying the fundamental principles of reality. By mastering the art of aligning these elements and harnessing their energy, readers can forge a path toward unbridled success.

Throughout the book, we'll explore different techniques and tips for using Feng Shui to promote success in various areas of our lives. This includes practical advice on how to arrange furniture and decor to optimize energy flow, as well as more spiritual practices such as meditation and visualization. By combining these techniques and applying them consistently, readers can create a harmonious and supportive environment that encourages success and fulfillment in all aspects of life.

History of Feng Shui

The chronicle of Feng Shui, as expounded upon within the context of a volume on the theme of success, delves into the genesis and metamorphosis of this timeless Chinese art and science. Hailing from the Zhou

Dynasty over 3,000 years ago, Feng Shui emerged as an approach to ascertain propitious locations for human habitation and interment. The volume meticulously unravels the intricate narrative of Feng Shui's progression, interlacing accounts of sagacity, ingenuity, and adaptation that have molded its contemporary significance.

During its infancy, Feng Shui chiefly revolved around geomancy or earth divination, discerning propitious sites by interpreting terrestrial energy patterns. The volume elucidates the indispensable role played by early Chinese celestial observers and diviners in crafting the foundational tenets of Feng Shui, drawing on astral insights to decode favorable alignments and arrangements.

The narrative ventures into the Han Dynasty, emphasizing the advent of Lo Shu Square and Bagua, two essential concepts that catalyzed a quantum leap in the maturation of Feng Shui. These advancements empowered practitioners to chart the circulation of Qi in man-made environments, utilizing the vigor of the five elements to balance the interplay of Yin and Yang energies optimally.

The Tang and Song Dynasties witnessed the zenith of Feng Shui, with its doctrines becoming deeply embedded within Chinese customs and architectural practices. The volume accentuates the sway of eminent Feng Shui adepts from this epoch, such as Yang Yun-sung and Wang Chih, whose erudite contributions reverberate in modern applications.

In the current era, Feng Shui transcends geographic and cultural frontiers, captivating a worldwide following in pursuit of equilibrium, abundance, and achievement. The volume investigates the amalgamation of conventional and modern methodologies, delineating the blending of Western architectural and design precepts with the venerable doctrines of Feng Shui.

This Feng Shui narrative, predicated on the subject of success, offers an immersive expedition through historical epochs, elucidating the trajectory of the age-old wisdom that has withstood the passage of time. By examining its inception and tracing its evolution, the volume unveils the key to unlocking triumph by synergizing with the natural order, epitomizing the quintessence of this enduring philosophy.

A Journey Through Time

This erudite Feng Shui tome, centered on the theme of prosperity and achievement, embarks on a comprehensive exploration of the diverse schools and methodologies that have emerged over time. It meticulously dissects each approach, providing context and rationale for its distinct principles. The volume ultimately focuses on the most pragmatic and efficacious tenets for nurturing success, synthesizing various schools to generate a harmonious and powerful framework for contemporary application.

Form School: As the earliest and most primordial branch, the Form School underscores the paramountcy of landscapes and topography in modulating energy flows. The volume delves into the concepts of the Four Celestial Animals and the interplay of natural formations, elucidating the potential of auspicious landforms to foster auspicious Qi and thereby engender prosperity.

Compass School: The Compass School, distinguished by its reliance on complex calculations and celestial influences, employs the Lo Shu Square, Bagua, and Flying Star techniques to determine ideal spatial arrangements. The tome examines these methods and their contributions to optimizing the circulation of Qi, underlining their pertinence to enhancing success.

Eight Mansions School: This approach accentuates the Kua number, an individual's unique energetic signature, to customize living spaces and maximize harmony with one's environment. The volume elucidates the process of determining auspicious and inauspicious sectors, underscoring the role of personalized Feng Shui in bolstering success.

Black Hat Sect (BHS) Feng Shui: Emerging from the syncretism of Tibetan Buddhism and classical Feng Shui, BHS emphasizes the Bagua Map and the application of symbolic enhancements or cures. The tome scrutinizes the efficacy of this intuitive and accessible school, evaluating its relevance to contemporary contexts and the pursuit of success.

New Age Feng Shui: An eclectic fusion of spiritual, psychological, and traditional Feng Shui principles, New Age Feng Shui focuses on decluttering, intentional design, and fostering positive energy. The volume dissects this modern approach, gauging its potential to nurture success and well-being.

Throughout the book, the author astutely extracts the most germane and effective techniques from these diverse schools, fashioning a holistic and versatile framework to cultivate success. By harnessing the strengths of each methodology and adapting them to contemporary sensibilities, the volume generates a potent amalgam of Feng Shui wisdom, empowering readers to elevate their fortunes and attain their aspirations.

Note: 'South' is always found at the top of the Bagua.

The Basics of Feng Shui for Success

Unveiling the Bagua Map:
A Key to Unlocking Success with Feng Shui

The Bagua Map, a fundamental concept in the realm of Feng Shui, serves as an essential guide to understanding the energy flow within our surroundings. Derived from the Chinese term "Ba" which signifies "eight" and "Gua" meaning "trigram," the Bagua Map comprises eight areas or guas, each symbolizing a distinct aspect of life. By harnessing the power of this ancient tool, we can enhance success in various facets of our existence.

To effectively utilize the Bagua Map, we must first gain a comprehensive understanding of its underlying principles. The map is typically portrayed as an octagonal grid or a square grid, with each section representing a unique gua. These guas are interconnected, signifying the harmonious balance of life's different elements. At the center of the map, the ninth area embodies the Earth element and unifies the surrounding guas.

The eight guas encompass the following life aspects:

1. Wealth and Prosperity
2. Fame and Reputation

3. Relationships and Love
4. Family and Health
5. Creativity and Children
6. Helpful People and Travel
7. Career and Life Path
8. Knowledge and Self-Cultivation

To optimize success using the Bagua Map, begin by overlaying the map onto your living or working space. The front door or entrance of the space should align with the bottom of the map. This placement allows you to identify the corresponding guas within your environment and make necessary adjustments to boost positive energy.

For instance, to enhance success in your career, focus on the Career and Life Path gua. By placing items that symbolize growth, such as a thriving plant, you can nurture the energy within this area. Additionally, incorporating the color black or water elements can further amplify the power of this gua.

Similarly, to attract wealth and prosperity, concentrate on the corresponding gua by placing items that signify abundance, such as a money tree or a bowl of coins. Utilizing the colors gold, purple, and green can also help to strengthen the energy within this area.

The Bagua Map, when used thoughtfully, can serve as a potent instrument in the quest for success. By recognizing the significance of each gua and making deliberate adjustments to our surroundings, we can harmonize the energy flow in our spaces, paving the way for a flourishing and prosperous future.

Harmonizing the Five Elements:
A Pathway to Success through Feng Shui

Feng Shui, an ancient Chinese practice, seeks to create balance and harmony within our surroundings to promote a thriving, prosperous existence. A cornerstone of this philosophy lies in the concept of the Five Elements: Wood, Fire, Earth, Metal, and Water. Each element carries its unique energy and qualities, which, when skillfully employed, can contribute to success in various facets of life.

To grasp the significance of the Five Elements and their connection to success, we must first understand their fundamental properties and interrelationships. The elements interact in two distinct cycles: the productive or generating cycle and the controlling or weakening cycle.

In the productive cycle, each element nurtures and supports the subsequent element:

1. Wood fuels Fire

2. Fire produces Earth

3. Earth creates Metal

4. Metal collects Water

5. Water nourishes Wood

Conversely, in the controlling cycle, each element dominates and weakens the subsequent element:

1. Wood depletes Earth

2. Fire melts Metal

3. Earth absorbs Water

4. Metal chops Wood

5. Water extinguishes Fire

To harness the power of the Five Elements for success, we must strive to achieve equilibrium in our living and working environments. This balance can be attained by incorporating the appropriate colors, shapes, materials, and objects that correspond to each element:

1. Wood: The element of growth and expansion is represented by the colors green and brown, vertical shapes, and materials such as plants, wooden furniture, or bamboo.

2. Fire: The element of passion and transformation is represented by the colors red, orange, and purple, triangular shapes, and materials such as candles, lights, or fireplaces.

3. Earth: The element of stability and grounding is represented by the colors yellow, beige, earth tones, square shapes, and materials such as ceramics, stones, or bricks.

4. Metal: The element of strength and clarity is represented by the colors of white and metallic shades, circular shapes, and materials such as metal objects, sculptures, or mirrors.

5. Water: The element of fluidity and wisdom is represented by the colors blue and black, wavy shapes, and materials such as fountains, aquariums, or images of water.

By attentively integrating the Five Elements in our spaces, we can foster a harmonious energy flow that promotes success in diverse areas of life, including health, wealth, relationships, and personal growth. The key lies in recognizing the influence of each element and tailoring our environments to create a stable, nurturing atmosphere that paves the way for a prosperous, fulfilling future.

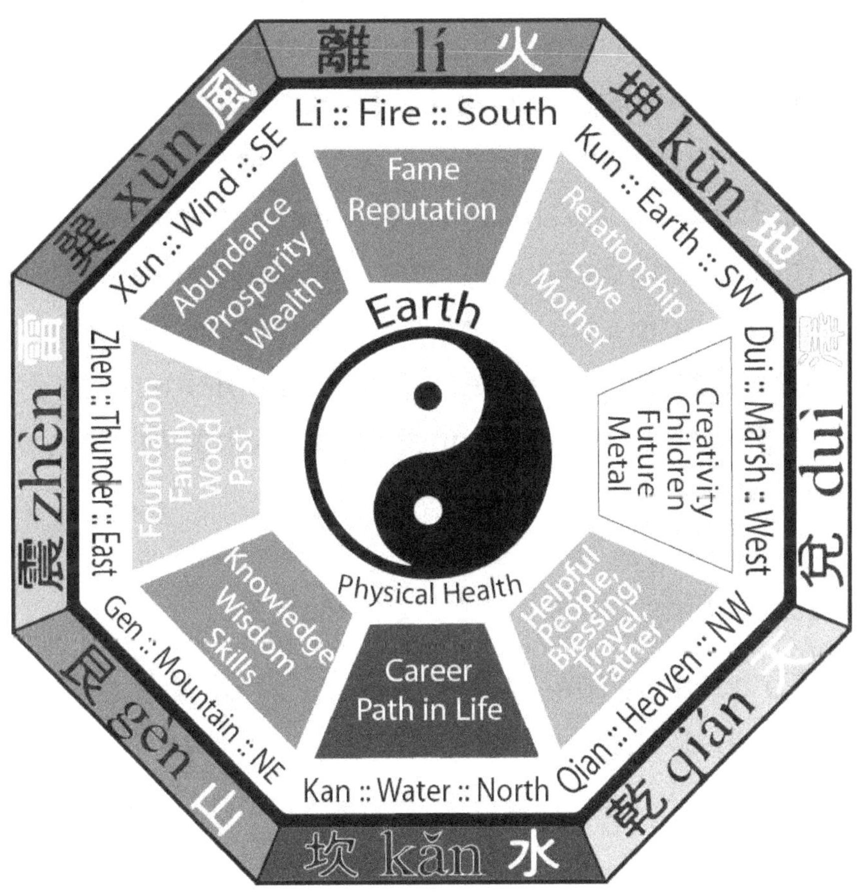

Note: 'South' is always found at the top of the Bagua.

Feng Shui Tips for Your Office or Workplace

Pathway to Prosperity: A Comprehensive Guide to Implementing Feng Shui Principles for a Successful Workspace

The time-honored Chinese wisdom of Feng Shui, a philosophical system that orchestrates the flow of energy, or "chi," in our surroundings, offers a transformative approach to enriching our lives on personal and professional levels. By incorporating Feng Shui tenets, one can cultivate a workspace that nurtures prosperity and triumph. "Pathway to Prosperity" provides a comprehensive guide to implementing Feng Shui principles to engender a thriving professional environment.

Understanding Chi and Its Significance:

To harness the power of Feng Shui, it is crucial to comprehend the essence of chi, the life force that pervades the cosmos. By fostering the harmonious circulation of chi within a workspace, one can bolster productivity and well-being. This understanding will serve as a foundation for effectively implementing Feng Shui principles and nurturing success.

Utilizing the Bagua Map and Cardinal Directions:

Feng Shui relies on the Bagua Map, an indispensable tool for discerning energy sectors within a space, and the significance of cardinal directions. Learn to navigate the Bagua Map and orient your workspace to harness the power of directional forces. By aligning your workspace with auspicious energy sectors, you can bolster your professional trajectory.

Strategically Arranging Furniture for Success:

The art of selecting and arranging furniture is essential for creating an ergonomic and energetically harmonious workspace. Discover how the optimal placement of desks, chairs, and other vital elements can facilitate focus, collaboration, and inspiration, ultimately contributing to professional success.

Crafting an Ambiance of Triumph with Color, Light, and Texture:

The influence of color, light, and texture on a workspace's energy and ambiance cannot be underestimated. Receive guidance on choosing palettes and illumination that invigorate and inspire, as well as incorporating tactile elements that engender a sense of balance and tranquility.

Incorporating Plants, Symbols, and Artifacts to Attract Success and Prosperity:

Plants, symbols, and artifacts hold the power to attract success and prosperity. Uncover the secrets of selecting and placing auspicious elements that bolster the potency of your workspace's energy and imbue it with an aura of triumph.

"Pathway to Prosperity" offers a comprehensive and invaluable guide to implementing Feng Shui principles in your workspace. By harnessing the ancient wisdom of Feng Shui and channeling the life-affirming energy of chi, you can create a workspace that fosters professional growth, success, and prosperity.

Envisioning Success: Enhancing Desk Placement, Lighting, and Decor with Feng Shui Principles for a Prosperous Workspace

Creating a prosperous workspace is pivotal to professional success, and the ancient Chinese practice of Feng Shui offers invaluable insights to achieve this goal. "Envisioning Success" delves into the art of optimizing desk placement, lighting, and decor by incorporating Feng Shui principles, thereby nurturing an environment conducive to achievement and growth.

Optimal Desk Placement for Success:

The position of your desk plays a crucial role in harnessing positive energy and promoting productivity. Adhere to the following suggestions to optimize your desk placement:

1. Position your desk to face the room's entrance or a window, allowing you to benefit from incoming energy.

2. Avoid placing your desk directly opposite the door or under overhead beams, as these locations can hinder the flow of chi.

3. Ensure that you have a solid wall behind you, which represents stability and support.

Illuminating Your Workspace for Triumph:

Lighting significantly impacts the ambiance and energy of a workspace. Follow these recommendations to create an invigorating atmosphere:

1. Maximize natural light by keeping windows clean and unobstructed.

2. Employ layered lighting, including ambient, task, and accent lights, to create a balanced and harmonious environment.

3. Choose warm, soft light sources that evoke a sense of comfort and inspiration.

Decor for Prosperity and Success:

The decor of your workspace can contribute to a sense of balance, motivation, and prosperity. Consider these suggestions to enhance your workspace's decor:

1. Incorporate colors that evoke success and productivity, such as shades of green, blue, or earth tones.

2. Display artwork that reflects your aspirations and inspires motivation, such as images of landscapes, water, or symbols of abundance.

3. Introduce plants, such as bamboo or money trees, which are believed to attract wealth and positive energy.

4. Position auspicious symbols, like the Laughing Buddha or dragon, in the wealth and career sectors of your workspace as defined by the Bagua Map.

"Envisioning Success" provides a comprehensive guide to enhancing desk placement, lighting, and decor using Feng Shui principles for a thriving workspace. By embracing these suggestions and cultivating an environment that fosters professional growth, you can pave the way for success and prosperity in your career.

Synergy Unveiled: Harnessing Feng Shui Principles to Amplify Communication and Teamwork for Success

Effective communication and teamwork are vital components of a thriving professional environment. By employing the ancient wisdom of Feng Shui, you can create a workspace that fosters collaboration and synergy, ultimately propelling your team toward success. "Synergy Unveiled" offers valuable tips for utilizing Feng Shui principles to enhance communication and teamwork within your organization.

1. Open Layout for Unobstructed Energy Flow:
   An open layout encourages the free flow of chi, promoting positive energy and interaction among team members. To create a harmonious workspace:
   - Arrange workstations in a way that minimizes barriers and allows team members to maintain visual contact.
   - Avoid overcrowding by providing ample space for movement and collaboration.

- Ensure that pathways are clear and unobstructed, allowing for easy communication and interaction.

2. Collaborative Seating Arrangements: Strategic seating arrangements can significantly impact team dynamics and collaboration. To foster effective communication and teamwork:
   - Opt for round or oval-shaped tables, which encourage open dialogue and a sense of equality among team members.
   - Position seats at an equal distance from each other to promote balance and inclusiveness.
   - Avoid seating arrangements that create a hierarchy, as they may hinder open communication.

3. Enhancing Communication with Colors and Elements: Colors and elements play a vital role in stimulating communication and collaboration. To create an environment that fosters teamwork:
   - Incorporate blue and green hues, which are associated with the water element, and stimulate open communication.
   - Use metallic accents or artwork that represent the metal element, as it promotes clarity and focuses in discussions.

- Balance the workspace with earth tones, which evoke stability and grounding, enabling team members to work harmoniously.

4. Encouraging Teamwork with Symbolic Decor: Strategically placed decor can inspire team members and strengthen the sense of unity. To enhance teamwork through symbolic decor:

   - Display images or artwork representing collaboration, such as a group of birds or people working together.
   - Place crystals, like rose quartz or amethyst, in common areas to promote positive energy and harmonious relationships.
   - Incorporate plants, such as bamboo or snake plants, which not only purify the air but also symbolize growth and adaptability.

"Synergy Unveiled" provides valuable insights into utilizing Feng Shui principles to amplify communication and teamwork for professional success. By embracing these tips and creating a balanced, harmonious workspace, you can pave the way for enhanced collaboration and synergy, ultimately propelling your team towards greater achievements.

Feng Shui Tips for Your Home

Harmonious Haven: Cultivating Success through Feng Shui Principles in Your Home

Feng Shui, an ancient Chinese discipline, encompasses the harmonization of energy flows within an environment to promote well-being, prosperity, and accomplishment. To effectively implement Feng Shui principles in your domicile to achieve success, consider the following guidelines:

1. Declutter and Reorganize: The initial step in cultivating a propitious atmosphere is to remove any disarray or clutter. Extricate superfluous items, and arrange your belongings meticulously, enabling energy to circulate unimpededly.

2. Front Door Fortuity: The entrance to your dwelling holds paramount importance, as it is the primary conduit through which energy, or "chi," flows. Ensure that your front door is unobstructed, visually appealing, and in optimal condition. Integrate auspicious colors, such as red or black, to attract prosperity.

3. Command Position: Position essential furniture, such as your bed, desk, and seating arrangements, to face the entryway without being in direct alignment with it. This commanding stance facilitates a sense of control and empowerment, fostering success.

4. Balance of Elements: Incorporate the five elements of Feng Shui - wood, fire, earth, metal, and water - in each room to create a harmonious, dynamic ambiance. Utilize colors, shapes, and materials that represent these elements to foster equilibrium and encourage productive energy.

5. Auspicious Symbols: Adorn your space with symbols of success, such as a dragon, phoenix, or horse. These emblematic representations serve as reminders and attractors of triumphant energy.

6. Enhance the Wealth and Career Sectors: The Bagua map, a fundamental Feng Shui tool, delineates your home's distinct energy areas. Pinpoint the wealth and career zones, and embellish these sections with auspicious colors, plants, and artwork to stimulate prosperity and professional growth.

7. Encourage Flowing Water: Water elements, such as fountains or fish tanks, symbolize wealth and abundance. Position these features in suitable locations, such as the wealth sector, to attract financial success and foster a serene atmosphere.

8. Sustain Greenery: Intersperse your residence with verdant plants, which signify growth, vitality, and progress. These botanical additions purify the air and enliven the environment, facilitating a thriving space.

By meticulously applying these Feng Shui principles, you can transform your abode into a sanctuary that nurtures success, well-being, and fulfillment.

Invigorating Ambiance: Boosting Success by Optimizing Energy Flow with Feng Shui

1. Unhindered Pathways: Ensure that hallways, doorways, and passages remain free from obstructions, allowing energy to circulate seamlessly. Arrange furniture in a manner that facilitates ease of movement and avoids creating barriers or dead ends.

2. Adequate Illumination: Embrace natural light, as it is a vital component of positive energy. Remove obstructions from windows, and utilize sheer curtains or blinds to modulate sunlight. Additionally, employ varied lighting options, such as ambient, task, and accent lights, to establish a radiant, inviting atmosphere.

3. Artful Curvature: Incorporate curvilinear shapes and designs in your home's layout, furniture, and accessories. Rounded edges and sinuous patterns promote the smooth flow of energy, while sharp angles and corners can generate stagnant or aggressive energy.

4. Mirrors and Reflections: Tactfully placed mirrors can magnify light, amplify space, and stimulate energy flow. Utilize mirrors in dimly lit or cramped areas, as well as in the wealth and career sectors, to reinforce positive energy and manifest success.

5. The Power of Fragrance: Introduce pleasant aromas through natural means, such as essential oils, incense, or scented candles. Aromatic elements can rejuvenate the atmosphere, purify energy, and elevate your mood.

6. Geomantic Harmony: Align your home with auspicious land formations and neighboring structures. Observe the surrounding environment for potential energy disruptors, such as buildings, roads, or natural elements, and employ Feng Shui cures to mitigate any adverse influences.

7. Spatial Segregation: Separate spaces for work, rest, and leisure to establish clear energetic boundaries. Designating distinct areas for various activities fosters focus, relaxation, and productivity, contributing to a well-balanced life.

8. Regular Energy Cleansing: Periodically refresh your home's energy through purifying rituals, such as smudging with sage, diffusing purifying essential oils, or employing sound therapy with bells or singing bowls. Consistent energy maintenance facilitates a vibrant, supportive atmosphere.

By conscientiously implementing these recommendations, you can invigorate the flow of energy within your domicile, fostering a nurturing environment conducive to success and overall well-being.

Holistic Harmony: Fortifying Health and Relationships for Success with Feng Shui

1. Energetic Sanctum: Designate a dedicated space for relaxation and rejuvenation, where you can meditate, practice yoga, or engage in other restorative activities. This sanctuary will support your physical and emotional well-being, fostering a balanced foundation for success.

2. Nourishing Nourishment: The kitchen symbolizes health and abundance in Feng Shui. Maintain cleanliness, organization, and functionality within this space. Introduce vibrant colors and fresh plants to promote vitality and ensure a nourishing atmosphere.

3. Restorative Slumber: Prioritize the bedroom as a haven for rest and rejuvenation. Employ calming colors, soft lighting, and minimal clutter to encourage relaxation. Position your bed with a clear view of the door, yet not in direct alignment, to foster a sense of security and equilibrium.

4. Harmonious Partnerships: Enhance the relationship sector of your home, as indicated by the Bagua map, with elements that promote love and partnership. Display pairs of objects, affectionate artwork, and warm colors to foster an atmosphere of unity and connection.

5. Balanced Yin and Yang: Embrace the complementary forces of yin (feminine, passive) and yang (masculine, active) throughout your home. This balance will encourage harmonious interactions and support overall well-being.

6. Tranquil Bathing Spaces: Treat your bathroom as a sanctuary for cleansing and renewal. Maintain cleanliness, declutter regularly, and incorporate soothing colors, plants, and natural elements to establish an oasis of tranquility.

7. Engaging Social Spaces: Arrange living and dining areas to encourage interaction and connection. Utilize circular or oval-shaped furniture, comfortable seating, and inviting colors to create welcoming environments for gatherings and conversation.

8. Personalized Health and Relationship Enhancers: Identify specific elements or symbols that resonate with your intentions for health and relationships. Integrate these personal emblems throughout your home to reinforce your commitment to nurturing these aspects of your life.

By diligently applying these Feng Shui tips, you can cultivate an environment that nurtures health and relationships, laying a robust foundation for personal and professional success.

Feng Shui Tips for Your Finances

Prosperous Pathways: Elevating Your Financial Fortunes through Feng Shui

Feng Shui, the ancient Chinese art of harmonizing one's surroundings, can be a potent tool for enhancing your financial prosperity and achieving success. By applying specific principles and adjustments, you can create an environment that attracts wealth and abundance. The following suggestions will guide you in optimizing your home's energy flow to foster financial growth:

1. Tidy and Organize: Begin by decluttering and organizing your living space. Eliminate unnecessary items and create a clean, orderly environment. This process allows positive energy, or "chi," to flow freely, fostering an atmosphere conducive to financial growth.

2. Prioritize the Entrance: The front door is the primary portal through which energy enters your home. Ensure it is in good condition, unobstructed, and visually appealing. Incorporate auspicious colors, such as red or black, to symbolize wealth and abundance.

3. Enhance the Wealth Sector: Utilize the Bagua map, an essential Feng Shui tool, to locate the wealth sector within your home. Once identified, activate and enhance this area with elements that represent prosperity, such as plants, crystals, or artwork depicting abundance.

4. Employ Auspicious Symbols: Integrate symbols of wealth and prosperity into your home decors, such as coins, money frogs, or sailing ships. These emblematic representations serve as visual reminders and energy attractors for financial success.

5. Water Element Activation: In Feng Shui, water is synonymous with wealth and abundance. Introduce water features, such as fountains or aquariums, in appropriate areas, like the wealth sector, to stimulate financial growth and cultivate a soothing ambiance.

6. Maintain a Functional and Prosperous Kitchen: The kitchen is a symbol of nourishment and abundance. Ensure that it is clean, well-organized, and fully functional. Keep the stove in optimal condition, as it represents the fire element and is associated with wealth generation.

7. Balance the Five Elements: Integrate the five elements of Feng Shui—wood, fire, earth, metal, and water—throughout your home to create a harmonious, dynamic environment. Use colors, shapes, and materials that symbolize these elements to attract wealth and maintain a balanced atmosphere.

8. Fortify Your Home Office: If you work from home or manage your finances from a dedicated space, apply Feng Shui principles to promote productivity and financial success. Position your desk in the command position, facing the door but not directly aligned with it. Incorporate organizational tools and inspiring artwork to cultivate a focused, prosperous workspace.

9. Encourage Generosity and Gratitude: Cultivate an attitude of gratitude and generosity, as these qualities attract abundance. Perform acts of kindness, donate to charitable causes, or create a dedicated space for a gratitude journal to reinforce these values.

10. Regularly Refresh Your Space: Periodically cleanse and refresh your home's energy through rituals such as smudging with sage, diffusing purifying essential oils, or implementing sound therapy. Maintaining a vibrant, supportive atmosphere is crucial for nurturing prosperity and well-being.

By meticulously applying these Feng Shui principles, you can create a harmonious, abundant living space that supports your financial goals and facilitates success. Remember that patience and persistence are key, as cultivating wealth and prosperity is an ongoing process. Embrace the journey and trust that the energy you create within your home will guide you toward a prosperous future.

Abundant Alchemy: Amplifying the Wealth Area of Your Home or Office through Feng Shui

1. Identify the Wealth Sector: Utilize the Bagua map, a fundamental Feng Shui tool, to pinpoint the wealth area within your home or office. Familiarize yourself with the layout and make a conscious effort to activate and enhance this sector.

2. Declutter and Organize: Eliminate any clutter, unnecessary items, or disarray within the wealth sector. Create a clean, orderly space that allows positive energy to circulate freely and fosters an environment conducive to financial growth.

3. Harmonious Color Palette: Integrate colors that symbolize wealth, prosperity, and abundance into the wealth area. Consider incorporating shades of green, gold, purple, or red to stimulate positive energy and attract financial success.

4. Elemental Balance: Ensure that the five elements of Feng Shui—wood, fire, earth, metal, and water—are well-represented within the wealth sector. Utilize colors, materials, and shapes that represent these elements to create a balanced, dynamic environment.

5. Prosperous Imagery: Adorn the walls of the wealth sector with artwork or images that evoke prosperity, abundance, and success. These visual representations can serve as powerful reminders and motivators for your financial aspirations.

6. Auspicious Symbols: Integrate symbols of wealth, prosperity, and good fortune into the wealth area, such as coins, money frogs, sailing ships, or dragon figurines. These emblematic elements can attract positive energy and reinforce your intentions for financial success.

7. Water Feature Activation: Water is associated with wealth and abundance in Feng Shui. Incorporate water features, such as fountains or aquariums, within the wealth sector to stimulate financial growth and promote a soothing, tranquil atmosphere.

8. Lush Greenery: Intersperse the wealth area with verdant plants, which signify growth, vitality, and progress. Opt for plants with round leaves or those that are traditionally considered auspicious, such as jade plants, money trees, or lucky bamboo.

9. Crystal Energy: Harness the power of crystals to attract prosperity and abundance. Position citrine, pyrite, or clear quartz crystals within the wealth sector to amplify positive energy and foster financial success.

10. Mirrors for Amplification: Utilize mirrors strategically to expand space, reflect light, and magnify positive energy. Place mirrors in the wealth area to reinforce prosperity and abundance.

11. Functional Furnishings: Select furniture that is both comfortable and functional for the wealth sector. Opt for pieces that encourage productivity and success, such as ergonomic chairs, spacious desks, or sturdy bookshelves.

12. Inviting Lighting: Illuminate the wealth area with a combination of natural light and artificial lighting options. Embrace sunlight, and utilize ambient, task, and accent lighting to create a warm, radiant atmosphere.

13. Aromatic Influence: Employ the power of scent to create a prosperous environment. Diffuse essential oils such as cinnamon, orange, or patchouli energize the wealth sector and attract abundance.

14. Motivational Messages: Display inspiring quotes, affirmations, or mantras within the wealth area to reinforce your financial goals and foster a success-oriented mindset.

15. Vision Board Creation: Design a vision board that showcases your financial aspirations and displays them prominently within the wealth sector. This visual reminder will help you maintain focus and motivation as you work toward your goals.

16. Financial Management Center: Establish a dedicated space for managing your finances within the wealth area. Organize your financial documents, budgeting tools, and investment materials to encourage systematic financial planning and responsible money management.

17. Wind Chimes for Energy Flow: Hang wind chimes in the wealth sector to stimulate the flow of positive energy and attract auspicious opportunities. Opt for chimes made from metal or wood, as these elements are associated with wealth and abundance.

18. Koi Fish Symbolism: Incorporate imagery or representations of koi fish, which are symbols of prosperity and good fortune in Feng Shui. Position koi artwork or sculptures within the wealth area to bolster your financial aspirations.

19. Gratitude and Generosity: Embrace an attitude of gratitude and generosity to attract abundance. Perform acts of kindness, donate to charitable causes, or create a dedicated space for a gratitude journal within the wealth sector to reinforce these values.

20. Periodic Energy Refreshment: Routinely cleanse and refresh the energy within the wealth sector through rituals such as smudging with sage, diffusing purifying essential oils, or implementing sound therapy. Maintaining a vibrant, supportive atmosphere is essential for nurturing prosperity and well-being.

21. Goal Visualization: Set aside time to visualize your financial goals and aspirations. Practice visualization exercises within the wealth area to align your intentions and energy with your desired outcomes.

22. Inspirational Reading Material: Curate a collection of books, articles, or other resources related to financial success and display them within the wealth area. Engaging with this material can provide valuable insights and motivation for your financial journey.

23. Networking and Connection: Foster a space that encourages networking and connection within the wealth sector. Arrange seating and furniture to facilitate conversation and interaction, creating an environment that promotes collaboration and support.

24. Celebrate Success: Acknowledge and celebrate your financial achievements, big or small, within the wealth area. Display awards, diplomas, or other symbols of success to remind yourself of your accomplishments and capabilities.

25. Ongoing Adaptation: Continuously evaluate the effectiveness of the Feng Shui adjustments within your wealth sector. Be open to refining and adapting your approach as needed to maintain an environment that supports your financial goals and aspirations.

By diligently applying these suggestions, you can create a harmonious, abundant environment within your home or office that bolsters your financial prosperity and facilitates success. Remember that patience and persistence are key, as cultivating wealth and abundance is an ongoing process. Embrace the journey and trust that the energy you create within your wealth area will guide you toward a prosperous future.

Magnetic Manifestation: Harnessing Feng Shui to Attract Abundance and Prosperity

Feng Shui, the ancient Chinese art of balancing the energies within one's surroundings, can be a powerful ally in attracting abundance and prosperity. By applying specific principles and practices, you can create an environment that supports your financial goals and promotes overall success. The following tips offer guidance on using Feng Shui to invite wealth and abundance into your life:

1. Clear the Clutter: Begin by decluttering your living space, removing unnecessary items, and creating a clean, organized environment. This process allows positive energy, or "chi," to flow freely, fostering an atmosphere conducive to abundance and prosperity.

2. Prioritize the Entrance: The front door is the primary portal through which energy enters your home. Ensure it is in good condition, unobstructed, and visually appealing. Incorporate auspicious colors, such as red or black, to symbolize wealth and abundance.

3. Enhance the Wealth Sector: Utilize the Bagua map, an essential Feng Shui tool, to locate the wealth sector within your home. Once identified, activate and enhance this area with elements that represent prosperity, such as plants, crystals, or artwork depicting abundance.

4. Balance the Five Elements: Integrate the five elements of Feng Shui—wood, fire, earth, metal, and water—throughout your home to create a harmonious, dynamic environment. Use colors, shapes, and materials that symbolize these elements to attract wealth and maintain a balanced atmosphere.

5. Incorporate Water Features: In Feng Shui, water is synonymous with wealth and abundance. Introduce water features, such as fountains or aquariums, in appropriate areas, like the wealth sector, to stimulate financial growth and cultivate a soothing ambiance.

6. Employ Auspicious Symbols: Integrate symbols of wealth and prosperity into your home decors, such as coins, money frogs, or sailing ships. These emblematic representations serve as visual reminders and energy attractors for financial success.

7. Maintain a Prosperous Kitchen: The kitchen is a symbol of nourishment and abundance. Ensure that it is clean, well-organized, and fully functional. Keep the stove in optimal condition, as it represents the fire element and is associated with wealth generation.

8. Create an Abundance Altar: Designate a dedicated space within your home for an abundance altar. Arrange symbols of wealth, prosperity, and gratitude in this area to reinforce your intentions and attract positive energy.

9. Energize Your Workspace: Apply Feng Shui principles to your home office or workspace to promote productivity and financial success. Position your desk in the command position, facing the door but not directly aligned with it. Incorporate organizational tools and inspiring artwork to cultivate a focused, prosperous workspace.

10. Cultivate Generosity and Gratitude: Embrace an attitude of gratitude and generosity, as these qualities attract abundance. Perform acts of kindness, donate to charitable causes, or create a dedicated space for a gratitude journal to reinforce these values.

By implementing these Feng Shui tips, you can create a harmonious, abundant living space that supports your financial goals and facilitates success. Remember that patience and persistence are key, as cultivating wealth and prosperity is an ongoing process. Embrace the journey and trust that the energy you create within your home will guide you toward a prosperous future.

Feng Shui Tips for Your Career

Ascendant Ambitions: Employing Feng Shui to Propel Your Career Success

Feng Shui, the ancient Chinese practice of harmonizing one's surroundings, can be an invaluable tool for those seeking to advance their careers. By applying specific principles and strategies, you can create an environment that supports your professional aspirations and fosters success. Here are several key tips for utilizing Feng Shui to propel your career forward:

1. Identify the Career Sector: First, locate the career sector within your home using the Bagua map, a fundamental Feng Shui tool. Once identified, concentrate your efforts on activating and enhancing this area to support your professional goals.

2. Clear the Clutter: Eliminate any clutter, disorganization, or unnecessary items from the career sector. A clean, orderly space allows positive energy to circulate freely and fosters an environment conducive to professional success.

3. Prioritize the Entrance: The front door is a crucial gateway for energy entering your home. Ensure it is in good condition, unobstructed, and visually appealing. Use auspicious colors, such as black or dark blue, which represent the water element associated with career advancement.

4. Embrace the Water Element: Integrate the water element, which symbolizes career growth and fluidity, into the career sector. Use colors, shapes, and materials that represent water, or introduce water features, such as fountains or aquariums, to stimulate professional development.

5. Balanced Lighting: Illuminate the career sector with a combination of natural and artificial light sources. Invite sunlight into the area and utilize ambient, task, and accent lighting to create a bright, inviting atmosphere that promotes productivity and focus.

6. Inspiring Imagery: Adorn the walls of the career sector with artwork or images that reflect your professional aspirations and goals. These visual cues can serve as powerful reminders and motivators for your career advancement.

7. Functional Furnishings: Select furniture that is comfortable, functional, and suitable for your professional pursuits. Opt for pieces that facilitate productivity, such as ergonomic chairs, spacious desks, or sturdy bookshelves.

8. Optimizing Your Workspace: Arrange your workspace to promote focus and efficiency. Place your desk in the command position, facing the door but not directly aligned with it. Keep the area clutter-free and organized, with all essential tools and materials easily accessible.

9. Networking and Collaboration: Foster an environment that encourages networking and collaboration within the career sector. Arrange seating and furniture to facilitate conversation and interaction, creating a space that promotes support and teamwork.

10. Affirmations and Goal Setting: Display inspiring quotes, affirmations, or mantras within the career sector to reinforce your professional goals and cultivate a success-oriented mindset.

11. Vision Board Creation: Design a vision board showcasing your career aspirations and display it prominently within the career sector. This visual representation will help you maintain focus and motivation as you work toward your objectives.

12. Ongoing Energy Maintenance: Routinely cleanse and refresh the energy within the career sector through rituals such as smudging with sage, diffusing purifying essential oils, or implementing sound therapy. Maintaining a vibrant, supportive atmosphere is essential for nurturing professional growth.

By diligently applying these Feng Shui principles, you can create a harmonious, empowering environment within your home that bolsters your professional aspirations and facilitates career success. Remember that patience and persistence are key, as cultivating a successful career is an ongoing process. Embrace the journey and trust that the energy you create within your career sector will guide you toward a fulfilling and prosperous professional path.

Ascendant Aspirations: Employing Feng Shui to Propel Your Career Forward

Feng Shui, the ancient Chinese practice of harmonizing one's surroundings, can be instrumental in fostering career success. By aligning the energies within your living and working spaces, you can create an environment that nurtures professional growth and achievement. The following guidelines detail how to use Feng Shui to advance your career and elevate your professional aspirations:

1. Identify the Career Sector: Utilize the Bagua map, a fundamental Feng Shui tool, to pinpoint the career area within your home or office. Familiarize yourself with the space and make a conscious effort to activate and enhance this sector.

2. Declutter and Organize: Remove any clutter, extraneous items, or disarray within the career sector. Establish a clean, orderly space that allows positive energy to circulate freely and fosters an environment conducive to professional growth.

3. Incorporate Water Elements: In Feng Shui, water symbolizes the flow of life and is closely associated with the career sector. Integrate water features, such as fountains or aquariums, to stimulate the flow of positive energy and encourage career progression.

4. Color Palette for Success: Employ colors that represent career growth, stability, and clarity within the career sector. Consider incorporating shades of black, blue, or white to energize the area and attract professional opportunities.

5. Establish a Functional Workspace: Design a workspace that is both comfortable and efficient within the career sector. Opt for ergonomic furniture, ample storage, and proper lighting to encourage productivity and focus.

6. Command Position: Arrange your desk in the command position, facing the door but not directly in line with it. This strategic placement enables you to see opportunities as they arise and symbolizes a proactive approach to your career.

7. Inspiring Imagery: Adorn the walls of the career sector with artwork or images that evoke your professional aspirations, such as representations of your desired career path, successful role models, or motivational quotes.

8. Embrace Natural Light: Ensure the career sector is well-lit, preferably with an abundance of natural light. Ample illumination stimulates positive energy and enhances focus and productivity.

9. Maintain Balanced Energy: Integrate the five elements of Feng Shui—wood, fire, earth, metal, and water—within the career sector to create a harmonious, dynamic environment. Use colors, materials, and shapes that represent these elements to promote balance and stability.

10. Network and Connection: Encourage networking and connection within the career sector by arranging seating and furniture to facilitate conversation and interaction. Cultivate an environment that promotes collaboration and support.

11. Set Clear Goals: Define your professional objectives and display them prominently within the career sector. This visual reminder will help maintain focus and motivation as you work toward your career aspirations.

12. Periodic Energy Refreshment: Regularly cleanse and refresh the energy within the career sector through rituals such as smudging with sage, diffusing purifying essential oils, or implementing sound therapy. Maintaining a vibrant, supportive atmosphere is essential for nurturing professional growth.

By diligently applying these Feng Shui principles, you can create a harmonious, supportive environment that bolsters your career aspirations and facilitates professional success. Remember that patience and persistence are key, as nurturing career growth is an ongoing process. Embrace the journey and trust that the energy you create within your career sector will guide you toward a fulfilling professional future.

Magnificent Merits: Boosting Reputation and Opportunities with Feng Shui

The art of harmonizing one's environment can be employed to enhance your reputation and increase opportunities for personal and professional growth. By implementing specific Feng Shui principles and techniques, you can create a living space that supports your aspirations and fosters success. Below are some valuable tips to help you harness the power of Feng Shui to improve your reputation and expand your opportunities:

1. Locate the Fame Sector: Utilize the Bagua map, a crucial Feng Shui instrument, to identify the fame and recognition area within your home. Familiarize yourself with this space and focus on activating and enhancing it to bolster your reputation.

2. Eliminate Clutter: Clear away any clutter or disorganization within the fame sector. Establish a clean, orderly environment that allows positive energy to flow freely, thereby fostering an atmosphere conducive to recognition and success.

3. Fire Element Activation: The fame sector is associated with the fire element. Incorporate fiery hues such as red, orange, or yellow into the area to ignite your reputation and attract growth opportunities.

4. Light Up Your Ambitions: Illuminate the fame sector with ample lighting to stimulate positive energy and enhance focus. Opt for warm-toned light sources, such as candles or lamps with soft, yellow bulbs, to evoke the fire element.

5. Display Your Achievements: Showcase your accomplishments within the fame sector by exhibiting awards, diplomas, or other tokens of recognition. These visual reminders will reinforce your capabilities and bolster your reputation.

6. Inspiring Imagery: Adorn the walls of the fame sector with artwork or images that represent your aspirations, such as symbols of success, influential role models, or motivational quotes. These visual cues can help attract opportunities and boost your self-confidence.

7. Inspiring Imagery: Introduce plants with upward growth, such as bamboo or tall, slender stalks, within the fame sector. These living elements symbolize growth, resilience, and success, and can contribute to an improved reputation.

8. Mirror the Success: Position a mirror within the fame sector to reflect symbols of success, such as your awards or inspiring artwork. This reflection will amplify the positive energy associated with your achievements and aspirations.

9. Positive Affirmations: Incorporate positive affirmations and empowering statements within the fame sector to reinforce your self-belief and confidence. Write these affirmations on decorative cards or notes and place them in prominent locations.

10. Maintain Energy Balance: Ensure that the five elements of Feng Shui—wood, fire, earth, metal, and water—are harmoniously integrated within the fame sector. Use colors, shapes, and materials that represent these elements to create a balanced environment that supports your reputation and opportunities.

11. Periodic Energy Refreshment: Routinely cleanse and refresh the energy within the fame sector through rituals such as smudging with sage, diffusing purifying essential oils, or implementing sound therapy. Maintaining a vibrant, supportive atmosphere is essential for nurturing your reputation and attracting opportunities.

By applying these Feng Shui tips, you can create a harmonious, supportive living space that bolsters your reputation and facilitates success. Remember that patience and persistence are key, as cultivating a favorable reputation and attracting opportunities is an ongoing process. Embrace the journey and trust that the energy you create within your fame sector will guide you toward a successful future.

Feng Shui Tips for Your Personal Growth

Flourishing Fulfillment: Harnessing Feng Shui for Personal Growth and Self-Improvement

Feng Shui, a time-honored practice rooted in Chinese tradition, offers a wealth of insights and techniques to foster personal growth and self-improvement. By applying specific principles, you can create a harmonious environment that supports your self-development journey. The following tips offer guidance on using Feng Shui to cultivate personal growth and self-improvement:

1. Identify the Personal Growth Sector: Utilize the Bagua map to locate the area within your home associated with personal growth, knowledge, and self-cultivation. Focus your efforts on activating and enhancing this space to support your self-improvement endeavors.

2. Create a Sanctuary: Transform the personal growth sector into a peaceful sanctuary for introspection, meditation, or relaxation. Incorporate comfortable seating, soft lighting, and calming elements such as plants or soothing artwork.

3. Remove Clutter and Distractions: Eliminate any clutter or distractions from the personal growth area.

Establish an organized, serene environment that allows positive energy to circulate and promotes mental clarity.

4. Embrace Earthy Tones: Introduce earthy colors, such as soft blues, greens, or browns, within the personal growth sector. These hues evoke a sense of grounding and stability, creating an atmosphere conducive to introspection and self-discovery.

5. Inspiring Literature: Curate a collection of books, journals, or other reading materials related to personal growth, spirituality, or self-improvement. Display these resources prominently within the space to encourage continuous learning and self-reflection.

6. Symbolic Representation: Decorate the personal growth sector with symbols that represent your aspirations and goals. These visual reminders can help maintain focus and motivation throughout your self-improvement journey.

7. Create a Vision Board: Design a vision board to display within the personal growth area, showcasing images, quotes, or affirmations that resonate with your goals and aspirations. This visual tool can serve as a powerful reminder of your intentions and help manifest your desires.

8. Integrate the Five Elements: Harmoniously blend the five elements of Feng Shui—wood, fire, earth, metal, and water—within the personal growth sector. Use colors, shapes, and materials that represent these elements to create a balanced and supportive environment.

9. Incorporate Natural Elements: Introduce natural elements such as plants, stones, or crystals to the personal growth sector. These elements can help ground and stabilize the energy, promoting a sense of calm and focus.

10. Cultivate Gratitude: Embrace an attitude of gratitude by creating a dedicated space within the personal growth area for a gratitude journal or jar. Regularly express appreciation for your achievements, lessons, and growth experiences.

11. Periodically Refresh Energy: Routinely cleanse and refresh the energy within the personal growth sector using methods such as smudging, sound therapy, or essential oils. Maintaining a vibrant and positive atmosphere is essential for nurturing personal growth and self-improvement.

By diligently implementing these Feng Shui principles, you can create a supportive environment that fosters personal growth and self-improvement. Remember that self-development is an ongoing process that requires patience, persistence, and commitment. Embrace the journey, and trust that the energy you cultivate within your personal growth sector will guide you toward a fulfilling and transformative path.

Cultivating Wisdom: Enhancing Knowledge and Self-Cultivation Areas for Success

An age-old practice originating from China offers valuable guidance for designing spaces that foster knowledge and self-cultivation. By applying its principles, you can create environments that support learning, reflection, and personal growth. Here are some suggestions for enhancing the knowledge and self-cultivation areas of your home or office:

1. Locate the Knowledge and Self-Cultivation Sector: Use the Bagua map to identify the area associated with knowledge and self-cultivation within your home or workspace. Focus on activating and enriching this space to encourage learning and personal growth.

2. Declutter and Organize: Clear away any clutter or disarray within the knowledge and self-cultivation sector. An orderly, clean environment promotes mental clarity and allows positive energy to flow freely.

3. Choose Calming Colors: Incorporate soothing, earthy hues, such as blues, greens, or browns, into the space to create a sense of grounding and stability. These colors contribute to an atmosphere that supports introspection and contemplation.

4. Create a Dedicated Workspace: Design a comfortable, functional workspace within the knowledge and self-cultivation sector. Opt for ergonomic furniture, proper lighting, and ample storage to encourage productivity and focus.

5. Display Inspiring Resources: Showcase books, journals, or artwork related to your interests, goals, or areas of expertise within the knowledge and self-cultivation sector. These resources can help maintain motivation and inspire continuous learning.

6. Incorporate Natural Elements: Introduce natural materials, such as plants, stones, or crystals, into the space. These elements can help ground and stabilize energy, fostering a sense of tranquility and focus.

7. Harmonize the Five Elements: Blend the five Feng Shui elements—wood, fire, earth, metal, and water—within the knowledge and self-cultivation sector. Use colors, shapes, and materials that represent these elements to create a balanced and supportive environment.

8. Encourage Reflection and Meditation: Designate a quiet corner within the space for reflection, meditation, or relaxation. Provide comfortable seating, soft lighting, and calming elements such as plants or soothing artwork to create a sanctuary for introspection.

9. Display Symbolic Imagery: Decorate the knowledge and self-cultivation sector with symbols that represent wisdom, growth, and learning, such as images of books, trees, or inspiring quotes. These visual cues can help attract knowledge and foster personal development.

10. Foster Networking and Connection: Arrange seating and furniture within the space to facilitate conversation and interaction. Create an environment that encourages collaboration, mentorship, and support among peers.

11. Regularly Refresh Energy: Periodically cleanse and refresh the energy within the knowledge and self-cultivation sector using methods such as smudging, sound therapy, or essential oils. Maintaining a vibrant, positive atmosphere is essential for nurturing learning and growth.

By implementing these Feng Shui suggestions, you can create a harmonious environment that supports knowledge acquisition, self-cultivation, and personal growth. As you embark on your journey of self-improvement, remember that patience, persistence, and commitment are crucial to achieving success. Trust in the power of the environment you've created to guide and inspire you along the path to self-discovery and accomplishment.

Ingenious Inspiration: Amplifying Creativity and Imagination with Feng Shui Techniques

This time-honored practice, with origins in China, provides a multitude of strategies and guidance for cultivating creativity and inspiration within your surroundings. By implementing its principles, you can design a space that encourages ingenuity, self-expression, and innovation. The following suggestions will help you apply these techniques to boost your creative energy and inspiration.

1. Identify the Creativity Sector: Utilize the Bagua map to locate the area within your home associated with creativity, imagination, and self-expression. Focus your efforts on activating and enriching this space to support your creative endeavors.

2. Clear Clutter and Distractions: Remove any clutter or disorganization from the creative sector. A clean, orderly environment allows positive energy to flow freely, promoting mental clarity and inspired thinking.

3. Embrace Playful Colors: Introduce playful, vibrant colors such as orange, yellow, or bright green into the creative sector. These hues evoke a sense of joy and curiosity, fostering an atmosphere that nurtures imagination and self-expression.

4. Curate Inspirational Elements: Display artwork, photographs, or other visual elements that inspire and uplift within the creative sector. These items can help maintain motivation and spark innovative ideas.

5. Encourage Experimentation: Designate a space within the creative sector for experimentation and exploration. Provide materials, tools, or resources that enable you to pursue new techniques, ideas, or forms of expression.

6. Create a Comfortable Workspace: Establish a comfortable, functional workspace within the creative sector. Choose ergonomic furniture, proper lighting, and ample storage to encourage productivity and focus.

7. Incorporate Natural Elements: Introduce natural materials, such as plants, stones, or crystals, into the creative sector. These elements can help ground and stabilize energy, fostering a sense of balance and calm amidst the creative process.

8. Balance the Five Elements: Harmoniously integrate the five Feng Shui elements—wood, fire, earth, metal, and water—within the creative sector. Use colors, shapes, and materials that represent these elements to create a balanced and supportive environment.

9. Encourage Collaboration: Arrange seating and furniture within the space to facilitate conversation and interaction. Create an environment that encourages collaboration, brainstorming, and support among peers.

10. Display Symbolic Imagery: Decorate the creativity sector with symbols that represent innovation, imagination, and self-expression, such as images of butterflies, paintbrushes, or inspiring quotes. These visual cues can help attract creative energy and foster personal development.

11. Periodically Refresh Energy: Routinely cleanse and refresh the energy within the creativity sector using methods such as smudging, sound therapy, or essential oils. Maintaining a vibrant, positive atmosphere is essential for nurturing creativity and inspiration.

By diligently implementing these Feng Shui tips, you can create a supportive environment that fosters creativity, inspiration, and innovation. Remember that the creative process requires patience, persistence, and a willingness to embrace the unknown. Trust that the energy you cultivate within your creativity sector will guide you toward a fulfilling and imaginative path.

Feng Shui Tips for Success in Relationships

Harmonious Bonds: Feng Shui Strategies for Nurturing Successful Relationships

This practice, deeply grounded in time-honored Chinese knowledge, provides essential perspectives and methods for cultivating balanced, thriving relationships. By adhering to its tenets, you can establish an environment that promotes love, communication, and connection. The following suggestions offer guidance on using these principles to foster success in relationships:

1. Identify the Relationship Sector: Utilize the Bagua map to locate the area within your home associated with relationships, love, and marriage. Focus your efforts on activating and enriching this space to support meaningful connections.

2. Declutter and Organize: Remove any clutter or disorganization from the relationship sector. A clean, orderly environment allows positive energy to flow freely, promoting harmony and balance within your relationships.

3. Embrace Warm, Inviting Colors: Incorporate warm, inviting colors such as pink, red, or peach into the relationship sector. These hues evoke a sense of passion, love, and warmth, fostering an atmosphere that nurtures emotional connections.

4. Establish Symmetry and Balance: Arrange furniture and decor in pairs within the relationship sector, symbolizing partnership and unity. Strive for symmetry and balance in your design choices to promote harmony within your relationships.

5. Choose Artwork and Decor Carefully: Display artwork or decorative elements within the relationship sector that reflect love, connection, and partnership. Avoid images depicting solitude or conflict, as they can negatively impact your relationships.

6. Encourage Open Communication: Arrange seating and furniture within the relationship sector to facilitate conversation and interaction. Create an environment that encourages open communication, support, and understanding among loved ones.

7. Incorporate Natural Elements: Introduce natural materials, such as plants, stones, or crystals, into the relationship sector. These elements can help ground and stabilize energy, fostering a sense of balance and harmony within your relationships.

8. Harmonize the Five Elements: Blend the five Feng Shui elements—wood, fire, earth, metal, and water—within the relationship sector. Use colors, shapes, and materials that represent these elements to create a balanced and supportive environment.

9. Opt for Soft Lighting: Choose soft, warm lighting within the relationship sector to create a cozy, intimate atmosphere. Avoid harsh, bright lights, as they can contribute to a sense of tension or unease.

10. Prioritize Comfort: Select comfortable, inviting furniture and textiles for the relationship sector. Opt for plush seating, soft pillows, and luxurious fabrics to create a space that invites relaxation and connection.

11. Regularly Refresh Energy: Periodically cleanse and refresh the energy within the relationship sector using methods such as smudging, sound therapy, or essential oils. Maintaining a vibrant, positive atmosphere is essential for nurturing successful relationships.

By diligently implementing these Feng Shui tips, you can create a harmonious environment that fosters love, communication, and connection. Remember that nurturing successful relationships requires patience, understanding, and a commitment to ongoing growth. Trust that the energy you cultivate within your relationship sector will support and enhance the bonds you share with loved ones.

Fostering Connection: Strengthening the Relationship Area in Your Home or Office with Feng Shui Principles

This time-honored Chinese tradition provides priceless wisdom and methods for cultivating thriving relationships. By implementing its tenets, you can establish an atmosphere that fosters love, communication, and connection. The following recommendations offer guidance on enhancing the relationship area of your home or office using these principles:

1. Identify the Relationship Sector: Utilize the Bagua map to pinpoint the area in your home or office related to relationships, love, and partnerships. Focus your efforts on activating and enriching this space to support meaningful connections.

2. Declutter and Organize: Remove any clutter or disorganization from the relationship sector. A clean, orderly environment allows positive energy to flow freely, promoting harmony and balance in your relationships.

3. Choose Warm, Inviting Colors: Incorporate warm, inviting colors such as pink, red, or peach into the relationship sector. These hues evoke a sense of passion, love, and warmth, fostering an atmosphere that nurtures emotional connections.

4. Create Symmetry and Balance: Arrange furniture and decor in pairs within the relationship sector, symbolizing partnership and unity. Strive for symmetry and balance in your design choices to promote harmony within your relationships.

5. Select Relationship-Themed Artwork and Decor: Display artwork or decorative elements within the relationship sector that reflect love, connection, and partnership. Avoid images depicting solitude or conflict, as they can negatively impact your relationships.

6. Foster Open Communication: Arrange seating and furniture within the relationship sector to facilitate conversation and interaction. Create an environment that encourages open communication, support, and understanding among loved ones.

7. Integrate Natural Elements: Introduce natural materials, such as plants, stones, or crystals, into the relationship sector. These elements can help ground and stabilize energy, fostering a sense of balance and harmony within your relationships.

8. Balance the Five Elements: Blend the five Feng Shui elements—wood, fire, earth, metal, and water—within the relationship sector. Use colors, shapes, and materials that represent these elements to create a balanced and supportive environment.

9. Opt for Soft Lighting: Choose soft, warm lighting within the relationship sector to create a cozy, intimate atmosphere. Avoid harsh, bright lights, as they can contribute to a sense of tension or unease.

10. Prioritize Comfort and Inviting Spaces: Select comfortable, inviting furniture and textiles for the relationship sector. Opt for plush seating, soft pillows, and luxurious fabrics to create a space that invites relaxation and connection.

11. Refresh the Energy Regularly: Periodically cleanse and refresh the energy within the relationship sector using methods such as smudging, sound therapy, or essential oils. Maintaining a vibrant, positive atmosphere is essential for nurturing successful relationships.

By implementing these Feng Shui suggestions, you can create a harmonious environment that fosters love, communication, and connection in both your home and office. Remember that nurturing successful relationships requires patience, understanding, and a commitment to ongoing growth. Trust that the energy you cultivate within your relationship sector will support and enhance the bonds you share with loved ones and colleagues alike.

Cultivating Harmonious Connections: Feng Shui Tips for Attracting and Maintaining Positive Relationships

This time-honored Chinese methodology offers priceless insights for drawing and preserving affirmative connections in your life. By adhering to its tenets, you can establish an environment that nurtures love, communication, and connection. Below are some suggestions for using these principles to foster and maintain positive relationships:

1. Harmonize Yin and Yang: Make certain that your living space strikes an equilibrium between Yin and Yang energies, promoting harmony and inviting affirmative relationships.

2. Unclutter Your Environment: Clear away clutter from your home, permitting energy to flow unobstructed. A clutter-free atmosphere enables transparent communication, understanding, and emotional openness in relationships.

3. Stimulate Chi Flow: Organize furniture and decor to create seamless, continuous pathways for Chi to circulate throughout your space, encouraging healthy, positive energy and bolstering strong connections with others.

4. Evoke Emotions with Colors: Incorporate warm, welcoming hues like pink, red, and peach within your living space. These colors elicit feelings of love and passion, aiding in attracting and sustaining positive relationships.

5. Emphasize Comfort: Opt for cozy furniture and plush textiles for your home, creating a hospitable environment that encourages connection and relaxation with loved ones.

6. Showcase Love Symbols: Display artwork or decorative elements symbolizing love and partnership, helping to invite supportive, affirmative relationships into your life.

7. Position Fresh Flowers: Introduce fresh flowers into your living space, signifying growth, vigor, and the blossoming of new connections. Replace them frequently to preserve fresh, dynamic energy.

8. Design a Tranquil Bedroom: Ensure your bedroom serves as a serene, restful haven devoid of distractions, fostering intimacy and connection with your partner.

9. Integrate Water Elements: Incorporate water features, like fountains or aquariums, into your living space. Water's association with emotions can help attract positive relationships and encourage emotional bonds.

10. Strategically Utilize Mirrors: Situate mirrors in your home to reflect affirmative energy and amplify your living space. Refrain from positioning mirrors directly opposite doors or windows, as this could cause energy to dissipate.

11. Cultivate Gratitude: Develop a mindset of gratitude for the relationships in your life. Expressing appreciation aids in attracting and preserving positive relationships, as it conveys a message of gratitude and love to the universe.

By implementing these principles, you can foster and preserve affirmative connections in your life. Remember that nurturing successful relationships demands patience, understanding, and an ongoing commitment to growth. Trust that the energy you cultivate in your living space will bolster and enhance your connections with loved ones and friends.

Feng Shui Tips for Mental and Emotional Well-being

Fostering Mental and Emotional Well-Being with Feng Shui Principles

This long-established Chinese custom offers significant wisdom for enhancing mental and emotional wellness through the organization and design of our living spaces. By observing its tenets, you can develop an environment that supports serenity, equilibrium, and personal growth. Here is a description of how to apply these principles to nurture mental and emotional well-being:

1. Cultivate Equilibrium: Harmonious surroundings are crucial for mental and emotional well-being. Aim for a balanced space by integrating the five elements (wood, fire, earth, metal, and water) and by synchronizing Yin and Yang energies.

2. Emphasize Tidiness: Clutter can hinder positive energy flow and lead to feelings of inertia and tension. Clearing your space of clutter allows energy to move freely, promoting clear-mindedness and emotional liberation.

3. Design a Tranquil Retreat: Allocate a space in your home for relaxation, meditation, and introspection. This haven should be free of distractions, fostering inner peace and deepening self-connection.

4. Optimize Illumination: Natural light is vital for mental and emotional wellness. Ensure your living area is well-lit with sunlight, and use gentle, warm lighting in the evenings to establish a comforting ambiance.

5. Incorporate Natural Elements: Blend natural components, such as plants, water features, and organic materials, into your living area. These elements help to connect you with nature and generate a sense of calm and tranquility.

6. Choose Calming Hues: Opt for soothing colors, like soft blues, greens, and earthy shades, for your walls and decorations. These tones induce peacefulness and can help alleviate stress and encourage relaxation.

7. Promote Positive Energy Movement: Position furniture and decor to create open pathways for energy to circulate effortlessly throughout your home. This stimulates a feeling of dynamism and vigor, contributing to overall mental and emotional wellness.

8. Apply Aromatic Therapy: Utilize natural fragrances like essential oils to establish a calming and invigorating atmosphere. Scents such as lavender, chamomile, and sandalwood can produce a calming effect on the mind and emotions.

9. Exhibit Uplifting Art: Select artwork that resonates with you and embodies your journey or goals. This can help to inspire and motivate you, nurturing a sense of purpose and well-being.

10. Foster Mindful Awareness: Cultivate mindfulness in your everyday life, attentively observing your thoughts and emotions without judgment. This can help establish a sense of internal harmony and serenity, supporting overall mental and emotional wellness.

By incorporating these principles into your living space, you can create an environment that bolsters mental and emotional well-being, fostering personal growth and internal balance. Keep in mind that nurturing a supportive environment necessitates time, effort, and a commitment to ongoing self-care. Trust that the energy you generate in your home will act as a foundation for mental and emotional well-being, assisting you on your path toward greater success and satisfaction.

Cultivating Wellness and Harmony: Enhancing the Health and Family Sectors with Feng Shui

The ancient art of Feng Shui provides a wealth of guidance for enriching the health and family sectors of your home or office. By meticulously arranging your environment and infusing it with positive energy, you can cultivate a space that fosters wellness, familial harmony, and success. Here are some suggestions for enhancing the health and family areas of your home or office:

1. Identify the Health and Family Sectors: Begin by pinpointing the Bagua sectors corresponding to health (center) and family (east). Utilize a Bagua map or compass to guide your efforts in these specific areas.

2. Balance the Five Elements: Strive for equilibrium among the five elements (wood, fire, earth, metal, and water) within the health and family sectors. This harmony will promote well-being and enhance relationships among family members.

3. Choose Rejuvenating Colors: Opt for shades that evoke feelings of tranquility and vitality, such as lush greens and earthy browns. These colors can help to create a nurturing atmosphere, fostering robust health and strong familial bonds.

4. Introduce Plants: Incorporate living plants into your space to symbolize growth, rejuvenation, and the nurturing aspect of the family. Select plants with rounded leaves and avoid those with sharp or pointed foliage.

5. Emphasize Natural Materials: Utilize furniture and decor crafted from natural materials, such as wood or bamboo. These elements embody the wood element, which is associated with family and vitality.

6. Create a Family Gallery: Dedicate a wall or corner to displaying cherished family photographs and mementos. This visual representation of family connections will help to strengthen bonds and promote positive energy within the space.

7. Encourage Open Communication: Arrange seating areas in such a way that they encourage open and comfortable communication among family members. This will foster a sense of unity and promote healthy dialogue.

8. Utilize Water Elements: Incorporate water features, such as fountains or fish tanks, to symbolize emotional flow and nourishment. This can help to foster harmonious relationships and emotional well-being within the family.

9. Prioritize Clutter-free Spaces: Remove clutter from the health and family sectors, enabling energy to circulate freely. A well-organized space encourages harmony and fosters a sense of balance within the family.

10. Cultivate a Peaceful Atmosphere: Strive to create a serene environment in the health and family areas, free from distractions and noise. This will encourage relaxation, healing, and emotional connection.

By implementing these suggestions, you can nurture a space that promotes physical well-being and fosters harmonious family connections. Remember, the journey to health and family success is an ongoing process that requires patience, care, and a commitment to maintaining a nurturing environment. Trust that the energy cultivated within your home or office will contribute to the well-being and success of you and your loved ones.

Harmonious Havens: Feng Shui Techniques for Stress Reduction and Relaxation

Feng Shui, an ancient practice originating from China, offers a wealth of knowledge and techniques for designing living spaces that foster relaxation and alleviate stress. By incorporating its principles into your home, you can create a sanctuary of serenity that supports a more balanced and peaceful lifestyle. Here are some tips for using Feng Shui to reduce stress and promote relaxation:

1. Embrace the Art of Decluttering: A cluttered environment can impede the flow of positive energy, contributing to feelings of chaos and overwhelm. By clearing your home of unnecessary items, you pave the way for tranquility and order, allowing positive energy to circulate freely.

2. Harmonize Yin and Yang Energies: Achieving a balance between Yin (soft, curved, and dark) and Yang (hard, angular, and bright) elements in your home encourages harmony and reduces stress. Integrate a mix of shapes, textures, and colors that embody both energies to create a sense of equilibrium.

3. Cultivate Calm with Color: Select soothing colors like soft blues, greens, and earth tones for your walls and decor. These hues evoke a sense of serenity, helping to create a peaceful atmosphere that fosters relaxation.

4. Design a Dedicated Relaxation Nook: Allocate a space in your home specifically for relaxation, meditation, or quiet reflection. This area should be free of distractions and designed to nurture inner peace, allowing you to disconnect from daily stressors and reconnect with your inner self.

5. Incorporate Nature's Beauty: Invite nature into your home by integrating plants, natural materials, and water features into your living space. These elements foster a sense of calm and tranquility, connecting you to the soothing essence of the natural world.

6. Illuminate with Intention: Harness the power of natural light during the day and utilize soft, warm lighting in the evenings. Proper lighting can significantly impact your mood and energy levels, cultivating a sense of relaxation and well-being.

7. Encourage Positive Energy Flow: Arrange furniture and decor to create open pathways for energy to flow smoothly throughout your home. This sense of movement and vitality helps combat feelings of stagnation and stress, promoting a more harmonious environment.

8. Engage the Senses with Aromatherapy: Employ essential oils and natural scents to create a calming atmosphere. Aromas like lavender, chamomile, and sandalwood possess soothing qualities, aiding in stress reduction and relaxation.

9. Display Inspiring Artwork: Curate a collection of artwork that evokes feelings of peace, serenity, or joy. Surrounding yourself with positive imagery contributes to a more relaxed and uplifting environment.

10. Develop Mindfulness Practices: Cultivate a mindfulness practice, such as meditation or deep breathing exercises, to help manage stress and maintain a sense of inner calm. This commitment to self-care can support your overall mental and emotional well-being.

By integrating these Feng Shui tips into your living environment, you can create a peaceful and stress-free sanctuary that promotes relaxation and well-being. Remember, achieving a balanced and harmonious space requires patience, effort, and ongoing self-care. Trust that the energy you foster in your home will support your journey toward greater success and fulfillment.

Putting it All Together

Pathways to Prosperity: A Recap of Feng Shui Tips for Success

This ancient Chinese practice, known for its time-honored wisdom, offers valuable insights into designing living spaces that promote success, harmony, and well-being. Here is a recap of the various tips for success discussed throughout this conversation, based on the principles of this practice:

1. Balance Yin and Yang energies: Create a harmonious environment by achieving equilibrium between Yin and Yang energies, promoting positive relationships and well-being.

2. Declutter your space: Remove clutter to facilitate the free flow of energy, encouraging clear communication and emotional openness.

3. Encourage positive Chi flow: Arrange furniture and decor to promote smooth and uninterrupted pathways for Chi, supporting strong connections and healthy energy.

4. Use colors to evoke emotions: Incorporate warm and inviting colors like pink, red, and peach to attract and maintain positive relationships.

5. Prioritize comfort: Select comfortable furniture and soft textiles to create a welcoming environment that fosters connection and relaxation.

6. Display symbols of love and partnership: Use artwork and decorative elements that represent love and partnership to attract supportive relationships.

7. Introduce fresh flowers: Use fresh flowers as symbols of growth, vitality, and the blossoming of new relationships. Replace them regularly to maintain fresh energy.

8. Create a restful bedroom: Design a peaceful, distraction-free sanctuary in your bedroom to encourage intimacy and connection with your partner.

9. Incorporate water elements: Add water features like fountains or aquariums to promote emotional connections and attract positive relationships.

10. Utilize mirrors strategically: Position mirrors to reflect positive energy and expand your living space, avoiding placements that cause energy to escape.

11. Practice gratitude: Cultivate an attitude of gratitude for your relationships, expressing appreciation and love to the universe.

12. Cultivate mental and emotional well-being: Establish balance, declutter, create a dedicated sanctuary, optimize lighting, incorporate nature, use soothing colors, encourage positive energy flow, utilize aromatherapy, and display inspiring artwork to foster mental and emotional well-being.

By applying these Feng Shui tips, you can create an environment conducive to success in all aspects of your life. Remember, nurturing success requires patience, understanding, and a commitment to ongoing growth. Trust that the energy you cultivate in your living space will support and enhance your personal and professional connections.

Integrating Feng Shui Tips for Success: A Step-by-Step Guide

Feng Shui, an ancient Chinese practice, offers a wealth of knowledge to help individuals design and arrange their living spaces to promote success, harmony, and well-being. However, implementing these tips can be overwhelming, especially for those new to the practice. This guide provides a structured approach to prioritizing and integrating Feng Shui tips into your life, ensuring that you derive maximum benefits from this time-honored tradition.

1. Assess Your Current Environment: Begin by examining your living or workspaces to identify areas that require improvement. Consider the flow of energy, clutter, the balance of elements, and the presence of natural materials. This assessment will help you determine which Feng Shui tips to prioritize.

2. Set Clear Goals: Define your objectives for each area of your life, including career, relationships, health, and personal growth. Having clear goals will help you focus your efforts and guide your application of Feng Shui principles.

3. Create an Action Plan: Develop a step-by-step plan for implementing Feng Shui tips, starting with those that address your most pressing concerns. Break down each tip into manageable tasks and set realistic deadlines for completion.

4. Prioritize Decluttering: Before delving into more complex Feng Shui principles, focus on decluttering your space. A clutter-free environment is essential for energy flow and serves as a foundation for further enhancements.

5. Implement Tips Gradually: Avoid overwhelming yourself by trying to implement all Feng Shui tips at once. Instead, integrate them gradually, allowing time to observe their impact and make adjustments as needed.

6. Seek Expert Guidance: If you're unsure about how to apply specific Feng Shui principles or if you encounter challenges, consider consulting a Feng Shui expert for personalized guidance.

7. Monitor Your Progress: Regularly evaluate the changes you've made to your environment, noting any improvements in your well-being, relationships, or success. This feedback will help you refine your approach and determine which tips have the greatest impact.

8. Maintain Balance and Harmony: As you integrate Feng Shui tips, ensure that you maintain a balance between the different elements and energies in your space. This equilibrium is crucial for cultivating an environment conducive to success and well-being.

9. Stay Flexible: Be open to adjusting your approach as your goals, priorities, or circumstances change. Flexibility is key to harnessing the full potential of Feng Shui principles.

10. Embrace Continuous Improvement: Treat the integration of Feng Shui tips as an ongoing process of refinement and growth. Regularly revisit your goals, assess your environment, and make adjustments to ensure that your space continues to support your success and well-being.

By following this structured approach, you can effectively prioritize and integrate Feng Shui tips into your life, fostering an environment that promotes success, harmony, and personal growth.

Cultivating Continuous Growth: Enhancing Your Feng Shui Practices Over Time

Feng Shui is a dynamic practice that requires ongoing attention and adjustments to ensure that your living and working spaces continue to support your goals and well-being. Here are some suggestions for maintaining and improving your Feng Shui practices over time:

1. Perform Regular Assessments: Schedule periodic evaluations of your space, noting any changes or areas that need attention. This proactive approach will help you address potential issues before they escalate and ensure that your environment remains harmonious.

2. Stay Informed: Continuously educate yourself about Feng Shui principles, techniques, and developments. This knowledge will empower you to make informed decisions about your space and implement new strategies as needed.

3. Embrace Seasonal Adjustments: As the seasons change, so too should your Feng Shui practices. Adjust your space to accommodate seasonal energies, colors, and themes, keeping your environment fresh and aligned with the natural world.

4. Be Mindful of Transitions: Life changes, such as career shifts, relationship developments, or family expansions, may necessitate adjustments to your Feng Shui practices. Be responsive to these transitions and adapt your space accordingly.

5. Maintain Open Communication: Encourage open dialogue with household members or coworkers about their experiences in the space. Their feedback can provide valuable insights into potential improvements and help you better understand the impact of your Feng Shui practices.

6. Monitor Your Goals and Priorities: Regularly revisit your goals and priorities, adjusting your Feng Shui practices as needed to support your evolving objectives.

7. Seek Inspiration: Stay inspired by exploring new sources of Feng Shui ideas and inspiration, such as books, blogs, workshops, or consultations with experts.

8. Cultivate a Supportive Community: Connect with others who share your interest in Feng Shui, exchanging tips, experiences, and encouragement. This support network can help you stay motivated and committed to your ongoing practice.

9. Experiment and Iterate: Be open to trying new approaches, techniques, or arrangements in your space. Continuously refine your practices, learning from your experiences and adapting your strategies to optimize your environment.

10. Practice Patience and Persistence: Recognize that cultivating a harmonious and supportive environment is an ongoing journey. Be patient with yourself and persistent in your efforts, trusting that your dedication to Feng Shui practices will yield meaningful results over time.

By incorporating these suggestions into your routine, you can ensure that your Feng Shui practices continue to evolve and support your well-being, success, and personal growth. Remember, Feng Shui is a dynamic process that requires continuous attention, adjustment, and learning. Embrace the journey and reap the rewards of your efforts.

Conclusion and Action Steps

The efficacy of Feng Shui as an ancient discipline goes beyond the mere improvement of one's living spaces, delving into realms of personal growth and triumph. When meticulously applied, this venerable art, with origins deeply rooted in ancient China, can cultivate harmony, well-being, and achievement within an individual.

Feng Shui's innate flexibility enables practitioners to tailor its principles to their unique lifestyles and personal inclinations. By exploring diverse techniques and maintaining receptivity to innovative concepts, individuals can constantly refine their Feng Shui expertise, unveiling new pathways to optimize their surroundings and nourish their inner selves.

Adopting Feng Shui also involves cultivating an enhanced sensitivity to the subtle energies that pervade our environments. This heightened awareness fosters a profound connection to the natural world and the vast cosmos, awakening our realization of the intricate interdependence within this magnificent web of existence. This newfound comprehension can elicit deep humility and gratitude for the enigmatic mysteries that pervade our lives.

Furthermore, the practice of Feng Shui encourages us to embrace a comprehensive view of success, extending beyond the bounds of material wealth or professional recognition. By acknowledging the manifold dimensions of success, we can strive to attain a harmonious balance between our physical, emotional, and spiritual well-being, thus paving the way for a more enriching and fulfilling life experience.

As we embark on our Feng Shui journey, it is essential to maintain an attitude of curiosity and open-mindedness. Approaching our practice with a willingness to learn and evolve enables us to continually refine our understanding of the art and its myriad applications. This ongoing process of introspection and personal growth can become a wellspring of inspiration, fueling our pursuit of success and self-realization.

In essence, the power of Feng Shui for success lies not only in its capacity to enhance our external environments but also in its potential to catalyze profound inner transformation. By assimilating its principles and nurturing a deep connection with the energies surrounding us, we can unlock the limitless potential within our hearts and minds. In doing so, we awaken to the boundless possibilities of existence, empowered to forge a path characterized by purpose, passion, and fulfillment.

In conclusion, the ancient art of Feng Shui possesses an extraordinary ability to foster success, harmony, and well-being across all facets of life. By incorporating its wisdom into our daily routines and remaining receptive to the ever-evolving dynamics of our existence, we can harness its transformative power to create a more vibrant, prosperous, and gratifying life experience. As we continue to delve into the depths of this ageless practice, we can rest assured that the power of Feng Shui will remain a steadfast ally on our journey toward self-discovery, growth, and the realization of our most cherished aspirations.

By embracing the tenets of Feng Shui, we embark on a lifelong journey of exploration and growth that transcends the mere optimization of our physical spaces. This potent practice has the potential to evoke a profound sense of interconnectedness, fostering enduring reverence for the delicate balance of energies that shape our lives and the world around us.

As we delve deeper into the realm of Feng Shui, we begin to perceive the underlying patterns that govern the flow of energy within our environments. This heightened awareness enables us to create spaces that are both visually appealing and energetically harmonious, imbuing our lives with a sense of tranquility and serenity.

Moreover, the practice of Feng Shui encourages us to embrace the cyclical nature of life, acknowledging the ebb and flow of fortunes and the inherent impermanence of existence. By cultivating a mindset of adaptability and resilience, we can navigate the vicissitudes of life with grace and equanimity, empowered to transform challenges into opportunities for growth and self-discovery.

At its core, Feng Shui serves as a potent reminder of the inextricable link between our inner and outer worlds. By nurturing our inner selves and creating harmonious environments that resonate with our unique energy signatures, we can facilitate a holistic approach to success that encompasses all aspects of our being.

Furthermore, the practice of Feng Shui encourages us to remain mindful of our intentions and aspirations, ensuring that our actions align with our higher purpose. In doing so, we can cultivate a sense of clarity and focus that empowers us to manifest our dreams and achieve our most cherished goals.

As we progress along our Feng Shui journey, it is essential to remember that the path to success is an ongoing process of learning, experimentation, and refinement. By remaining open to new ideas and approaches, we can continually hone our skills and deepen our understanding of this ancient art, unlocking ever greater levels of success and fulfillment.

Ultimately, the power of Feng Shui for success lies in its ability to inspire a profound sense of harmony, balance, and well-being that permeates every aspect of our lives. By integrating its principles into our daily routines and remaining attuned to the ever-shifting energies of our environments, we can harness its transformative potential to create a life of purpose, passion, and prosperity. As we continue to explore the rich tapestry of this timeless practice, we are reminded that the true essence of success lies in the cultivation of a life that is in harmony with our authentic selves and the world around us.

Action Steps for Feng Shui on the Topic of Success:

1. Assess your environment: Analyze the layout and design of your living and working spaces. Identify areas where energy may be stagnant or imbalanced and consider implementing Feng Shui remedies, such as

rearranging furniture or incorporating auspicious colors and symbols.

2. Embrace decluttering: Clutter can obstruct the flow of energy in your environment, leading to stagnation and potential obstacles to success. Regularly declutter and organize your spaces to promote harmony, clarity, and focus.

3. Set clear intentions: Reflect upon your goals and aspirations and set specific intentions for each area of your life. Use these intentions to guide your Feng Shui practice, ensuring that your actions align with your higher purpose.

4. Learn and apply Feng Shui principles: Study the core principles of Feng Shui, such as the Bagua Map, Five Elements, and Yin-Yang balance, and apply these concepts to your environment to create spaces that support your goals and well-being.

5. Nurture your inner self: Cultivate a regular self-care practice that includes activities such as meditation, exercise, and journaling to support your emotional, mental, and spiritual well-being.

6. Stay open to change: As you progress on your Feng Shui journey, remain open to new ideas and approaches. Continually refine your understanding and

application of the art to unlock greater levels of success and fulfillment.

7. Cultivate gratitude and mindfulness: Practice gratitude for the opportunities and blessings in your life and maintain mindfulness of the delicate balance of energies that shape your existence.

By taking these action steps and integrating the principles of Feng Shui into your life, you will create a powerful foundation for personal success and enrichment that transcends the mere optimization of your physical spaces. Embrace the transformative potential of this ancient practice and embark on a journey toward a life characterized by harmony, balance, and well-being.